SOLITUDE

SOLITUDE

Compiled by
Michael Joseph

STANYAN BOOKS

RANDOM HOUSE

A Stanyan book
Published by Stanyan Books,
8721 Sunset Blvd., Suite C
Hollywood, California 90069,
and by Random House, Inc.
201 East 50th Street
New York, N.Y. 10022

Library of Congress Catalog
Card Number: 72-81614

ISBN: 0-394-48216-6

Printed in U.S.A.
Designed by Hy Fujita

WE'RE ALL IN THE SAME BOAT . . .

. . . Solitude is essential to man.
All men come into this world alone;
all leave it alone.

— THOMAS De QUINCEY

I don't know anyone who isn't lonely . . .
You just learn to live with it.
You don't dwell on it.
That's the only way to handle it.

— JOAN CRAWFORD

Men fear silence as they fear solitude,
because both give them a glimpse of
the terror of life's nothingness.

— ANDRÉ MAUROIS

Did you ever watch people coming out of
a night club? There are few smiles
as a rule, and most faces are as grim as
when they went in. They are lost and
lonely, even in the midst of the crowd.

— BILLY GRAHAM

What's wrong with going places by
yourself? I do it all the time.

— AVA GARDNER

I give the fight up; let there be an end,
A privacy, an obscure nook for me,
I want to be forgotten even by God.

— ROBERT BROWNING

We are all, in the last analysis, alone.

— ANNE MORROW LINDBERGH

Dante was very bad company, and was
never invited to dinner. Michelangelo
had a sad, sour time of it. Columbus
discovered no isle or key so lonely
as himself.

— RALPH W. EMERSON

Thus let me live, unseen, unknown;
thus unlamented let me die; steal from
the world, and not a stone tell where I lie.

— ALEXANDER POPE

I dislike the bleak look of winter in a big
city, because it accents man's
natural loneliness.

— BURT LANCASTER

Loneliness, far from being a rare and
curious phenomenon, peculiar to myself
and a few other solitary men, is the central
and inevitable fact of human existence.

— THOMAS WOLFE

Until I truly loved, I was alone.

— CAROLINE NORTON

Why should we faint and fear to live alone,
since all alone, so Heaven has willed,
we die?

— JOHN KEMBLE

I have had many lonely hours.
Not all-alone-in-the-house,
that sort of thing, but in my thoughts
I've had many lonely hours.

— BETTE DAVIS

How insular and pathetically solitary
are all the people we know!

— RALPH W. EMERSON

It easeth some, though none it ever cured,
To think their dolor others have endured.

— WILLIAM SHAKESPEARE

Quiet to quick bosoms is a hell.

— LORD BYRON

Living alone will correct me of my faults,
for a man can do without his own
approbations in society, but he must
make great exertions to gain it when
he lives alone.

— SYDNEY SMITH

To fear a crowd, and yet fear solitude:
what a hateful predicament.

— XENOPHON

Solitude holds a cup sparkling with bliss
in her right hand, a raging dagger in
her left. To the blessed she offers her
goblet, but stretches toward the wretched
the ruthless steel.

— FRIEDRICH KLOPSTOCK

There is no man so miserable as he
that is at a loss how to use his time.

— SENECA

It is tormenting to fear what you
cannot overcome.

— AUSONIUS

Joy is a partnership,
    Grief weeps alone . . .

— FREDERICK L. KNOWLES

You need a formed character to
stand a solitude.

— AUSTIN O'MALLEY

All the misfortunes of men spring
from their not knowing how to live
quietly at home, in their own rooms.

— BLAISE PASCAL

The surest cure for vanity is loneliness.

— THOMAS WOLFE

In a real dark night of the soul it is always
three o'clock in the morning.

— F. SCOTT FITZGERALD

We walk alone in the world.
Friends, such as we desire,
are dreams and fables.

— RALPH W. EMERSON

Make voyages. Attempt them.
That's all there is.

— TENNESSEE WILLIAMS
Camino Real

We may get away by ourselves —
but we cannot get away *from* ourselves.

— BEVINS JAY

It (*Follies*) says very clearly that to be
emotionally committed to somebody is
very difficult, but to be alone
is impossible.

— STEPHEN SONDHEIM

In solitude the lonely man is eaten up by
himself, among crowds by the many.
Choose which you prefer.

— NIETZSCHE

Being alone is not something that one
can take or leave. We *are* solitary.
We may delude ourselves and act as
though this were not so. But how much
better to realize that we are so — yes,
even to begin by assuming it.

— RILKE

The owl is not considered the wiser
for living retiredly.

— THOMAS FULLER

Solitude is impracticable, and society
fatal. We must keep our head in the one,
and our hands in the other. The conditions
are met if we keep our independence,
yet do not lose our sympathy.

— RALPH W. EMERSON

Many people live alone and like it,
but most of them live alone and look it.

— GELETT BURGESS

The longest period of time in which a
human being has been totally isolated —
without sight, touch or hearing —
is 92 hours.

The times are not so bad as they seem.
They couldn't be.

— JAY FRANKLIN

What would a man do if he were
compelled to live always in the sultry heat
of society, and could never better
himself in cool solitude?

— NATHANIEL HAWTHORNE

All of the animals excepting man know
that the principal business of life is to
enjoy it.

— SAMUEL BUTLER

I was lonelier when I was married
than I am now, living alone.

— ALEXANDER DREY

My desolation begins to make a better life.

— WILLIAM SHAKESPEARE

Little do men perceive what solitude is . . .
For a crowd is not company;
and faces are but a gallery of pictures;
and talk but a tinkling cymbal where
there is no love.

— FRANCIS BACON

If a man be a coxcomb solitude is his
best school, and if he be a fool it is his
best sanctuary.

— ALEXANDER POPE

Eagles commonly fly alone;
they are crows, daws and starlings
that flock together.

— JOHN WEBSTER

One hour of thoughtful solitude may
nerve the heart for days of conflict.

— JAMES PERCIVAL

Why should I feel lonely? Is not our
planet in the Milky Way?

— HENRY DAVID THOREAU

If a word be worth one shekel,
silence is worth two.

— RABBI BEN AZAI

In solitude, where we are least alone.

— LORD BYRON

The good and wise lead quiet lives.

— EURIPIDES

It is better to be alone than in ill company.

— GEORGE PETTIE

He who has lived obscurely and quietly
has lived well.

— OVID

He leadeth me beside the still waters.

— PSALMS 23:2

What a commentary on our civilization, when being alone is considered suspect; when one has to apologize for it, make excuses. . . . Actually these are among the most important times in one's life — when one is alone.

— ANNE MORROW LINDBERGH

The great man is he who in the midst of the crowd keeps with perfect sweetness the independence of solitude.

— RALPH W. EMERSON

There is no such thing as solitude, nor
anything that can be said to be alone . . .
but God; who is His own circle and can
subsist by Himself.

— THOMAS BROWNE

Lost to virtue, lost to manly thought,
lost to the noble sallies of the soul,
who think it solitude to be alone.

— EDWARD YOUNG

I wish that every morning of my life
between May and October I had got out
of bed to see the summer dawn. What a
beautiful thing to see and be with . . .

— REX STOUT

No soul is desolate as long as there is
a human being for whom it can feel trust
and reverence.

— GEORGE ELIOT

The race is not to the swift,
nor the battle to the strong.

— ECCLESIASTES 9:11

I was never less alone than when
by myself.

— EDWARD GIBBON

Language has created the word
loneliness to express the pain of being
alone, and the word *solitude* to express
the glory of being alone.

— PAUL TILLICH

The strongest man in the world
is he who stands most alone.

— HENRIK IBSEN

I am never bored anywhere;
being bored is an insult to oneself.

— JULES RENARD

If I were a doctor and were asked for
my advice, I should reply: Create silence.

— SÖREN KIERKEGAARD

Depart from the highway and transplant
thyself in some enclosed ground, for it is
hard for a tree that stands by the wayside
to keep its fruit until it be ripe.

— JOHN CHRYSOSTOM

Is life worth living? It depends on the liver.

— SIR HERBERT BEERBOHM TREE

Be of good cheer.

— MATTHEW 14:27

If you think you're lonely, try being in
New York City without a friend.

— BESSIE LORRAINE BOLES

DON'T BE AFRAID . . .

When a man is alone he is safe.

— ALEXANDER DREY

I know that oft we tremble at an empty
terror, but the false phantasm brings
a real misery.

— JOHANN SCHILLER

The one thing I am most afraid of is fear.

— MONTAIGNE

Or in the night, imagining some fear,
How easy is a bush supposed a bear!

— WILLIAM SHAKESPEARE

Our instinctive emotions are those we
have inherited from a much more
dangerous world, and contain, therefore,
a larger portion of fear than they should.

— BERTRAND RUSSELL

Isn't your life extremely flat with nothing
whatever to grumble at?

— WILLIAM S. GILBERT

Girls who wear zippers shouldn't
live alone.

— JOHN VAN DRUTEN
The Voice of the Turtle

Some marriages require a daily dinner
guest—to fill up the void of loneliness.

— PAUL MURPHY

In Genesis it says that it is not good for a
man to be alone, but sometimes
it's a great relief.

— JOHN BARRYMORE

I am not surprised some people are bored
when they are alone, for they cannot
laugh if they are by themselves. Why not?
These people lack imagination.

— ARTHUR SCHOPENHAUER

I had as lief have their room as
their company.

— ROBERT GREENE

I hate a fellow whom pride or cowardice
or laziness drives into a corner, and who
does nothing when he is there but sit
and growl. Let him come out as I do,
and bark.

— SAMUEL JOHNSON

No girl who is afraid to stay home alone
in the evening should ever get married.

— ED HOWE

Talent is best nurtured in solitude.

— GOETHE

Loneliness is only an opportunity
to cut adrift and find yourself.

— ANNA SHANNON MONROE

A foundation of good sense and a
cultivation of learning are required to
give a seasoning to retirement and
make us taste of its blessings.

— JOHN DRYDEN

In solitude the mind gains strength,
and learns to lean upon itself; in the world
it seeks a few treacherous supports—
the feigned compassions of one,
the flattery of a second, the civilities of a
third, the friendship of a fourth;
they all deceive, and bring the mind back
to retirement, reflection, and books.

— LAURENCE STERNE

Conversation enriches the under-
standing, but solitude is the school
of genius.

— EDWARD GIBBON

The love of retirement has adhered to
those minds which have been most
enlarged by knowledge . . . Those who
enjoyed everything supposed to confer
happiness have been forced to seek
it in shades of privacy.

— SAMUEL JOHNSON

If a man write a better book, preach a
better sermon, or make a better mouse-
trap . . . the world will make a beaten
path to his door.

— RALPH W. EMERSON

Have you forgotten how nice it is that —

1. You can get into bed the minute you're home — and have a peanut butter sandwich for dinner.

2. When you're wide awake for no reason at four in the morning, you can turn on your bedside lamp and do your nails, put up a hem, read a book straight through.

3. You can collapse in bed all weekend — go without makeup or even without clothes.

4. You can postpone all housework until something *must* be done.

5. You can play your new record 82 times in a row without driving someone to the nut house.

6. You can burrow in with uninterrupted work from the office.

7. You can talk on the telephone for hours.

8. You can hide the phone under blankets and never answer.

9. You can sink up to your elbows in plants, paints, beads, clay, tile, sequins, yarn or any hobby that pleases you.

10. You can call up people and have a sudden party because you're in the mood — nobody to consult who may *not* be in the mood.

11. You can leave the radio or TV turned off for eight weeks, or play them non-stop.

12. You can have private conversations with your cat, dog, parakeet without somebody implying you're a nutburger.

13. You can eat loads of little green onions and garlic toast without driving anybody away.

14. You can sleep with the windows closed, or wide open.

15. You can do absolutely *nothing* for hours.

— HELEN GURLEY BROWN
Outrageous Opinions

These should be hours for necessities,
Not for delights; times to repair our nature
With comforting repose, and not for us
To waste these times.

— WILLIAM SHAKESPEARE
Henry VIII

I want to be left alone,
to work my own way.

—FRANK SINATRA

It is when a man is alone that he can work
on himself. It is in solitude that he must
correct his thoughts, driving out the bad
and stimulating the good.

— TOLSTOY

Fill a house with animals,
and you fill it with life.

— HUBERT De GIVENCHY

I really have perfect fun with myself.
Other people won't stop to look at the
things I want to look at or, if they do,
they stop to please me or to humor me.

— KATHERINE MANSFIELD

Shakespeare, Leonardo da Vinci,
Benjamin Franklin, and Lincoln . . . had
'loneliness' and knew what to do with it.
They were not afraid of being lonely
because they knew that was when the
creative mood in them would work.

— CARL SANDBURG

To judge rightly of our own worth we
should retire from the world so as to see
both its pleasures and pains in their
proper light . . .

— LAURENCE STERNE

Solitude, the safeguard of mediocrity,
is to genius the stern friend . . . He who
would inspire and lead must be defended
from travelling with the souls of
other men . . .

— RALPH W. EMERSON

The temple of our purest thoughts
is silence.

— SARAH J. HALE

Given three requisites — means of
existence, reasonable health, and an
absorbing interest — those years beyond
sixty can be the happiest and most
satisfying of a lifetime.

— ERNEST CALKINS

The best thinking has been done in
solitude. The worst has been in turmoil.

— THOMAS EDISON

By all means use sometimes to be alone:
Salute thyself; see what thy soul
doth wear.

— GEORGE HERBERT

It is the mark of a superior man that,
left to himself, he is able endlessly to
amuse, interest and entertain himself out
of his personal stock of meditations,
ideas, criticisms, memories, philosophy,
humor and what not.

— GEORGE NATHAN

It would do the world good if every man
in it would compel himself occasionally
to be absolutely alone. Most of the world's
progress has come out of such
loneliness.

— BRUCE BARTON

The happiest of all lives is a busy solitude.

— VOLTAIRE

Two are company — one is utter peace.

— ALEXANDER DREY

Our life, exempt from public haunt,
finds tongues in trees, books in the
running brooks, sermons in stones,
and good in everything.

— WILLIAM SHAKESPEARE
As You Like It

Solitude is one of the highest enjoyments
of which our nature is susceptible.

— LORD DELOREINE

If the mind loves solitude, it has thereby acquired a loftier character, and it becomes still more noble when the taste is indulged in.

— WILHELM HUMBOLDT

What sweet delight a quiet life affords.

— WILLIAM DRUMMOND

To live alone is an achievement — and vastly preferable to a bad marriage.

— KATHRYN MAYE

Oh, the pleasure of eating alone! — eating my dinner alone!

— CHARLES LAMB

There is a pleasure in the pathless woods;
there is a rapture on the lonely shore;
there is society, where none intrudes,
by the deep sea, and music in its roar.

— LORD BYRON

Far from the madding crowd's
ignoble strife.

— THOMAS GRAY

Anything for a quiet life.

— THOMAS MIDDLETON
(Title of a play)

Two Paradises 'twere in one
To live in Paradise alone.

— ANDREW MARVELL

I am monarch of all I survey
My right there is none to dispute.

— WILLIAM COWPER

That inward eye
Which is the bliss of solitude.

— WILLIAM WORDSWORTH

A man who can retire from the world has
a thousand advantages of which other
people have no idea. He is master of his
own company and pleasures . . .
all nature is ready for his view . . .
he can transport himself to the most
distant regions . . .

— HIBERNICUS' LETTERS

In the world a man lives in his own age;
in solitude in all ages.

— WILLIAM MATTHEWS

Happy is the man who lives contented
with himself in some retired nook.

— NICHOLAS BOILEAU

Parting is incvitably painful. . . . yet once
it is done, I find there is a quality to being
alone that is incredibly precious.
Life rushes back into the void, richer,
more vivid, fuller than before.

— ANNE MORROW LINDBERGH

Silence is the rest of the mind, and is to the spirit what sleep is to the body.

— WILLIAM PENN

My notions of life are much the same as they are about travelling; there is a good deal of amusement on the road, but, after all, one wants to be at rest.

— ROBERT SOUTHEY

I would rather sit on a pumpkin and have it all to myself than be crowded on a velvet cushion.

— HENRY DAVID THOREAU

Converse with men makes sharp the
glittering wit, but God to man doth
speak in solitude.

— JOHN STUART BLACKIE

Better is a handful with quietness,
than both the hands full with travail
and vexation of spirit.

— ECCLESIASTES 4:6

He whom God hath gifted with the love of
retirement possesses, as it were,
an extra sense.

— EDWARD BULWER-LYTTON

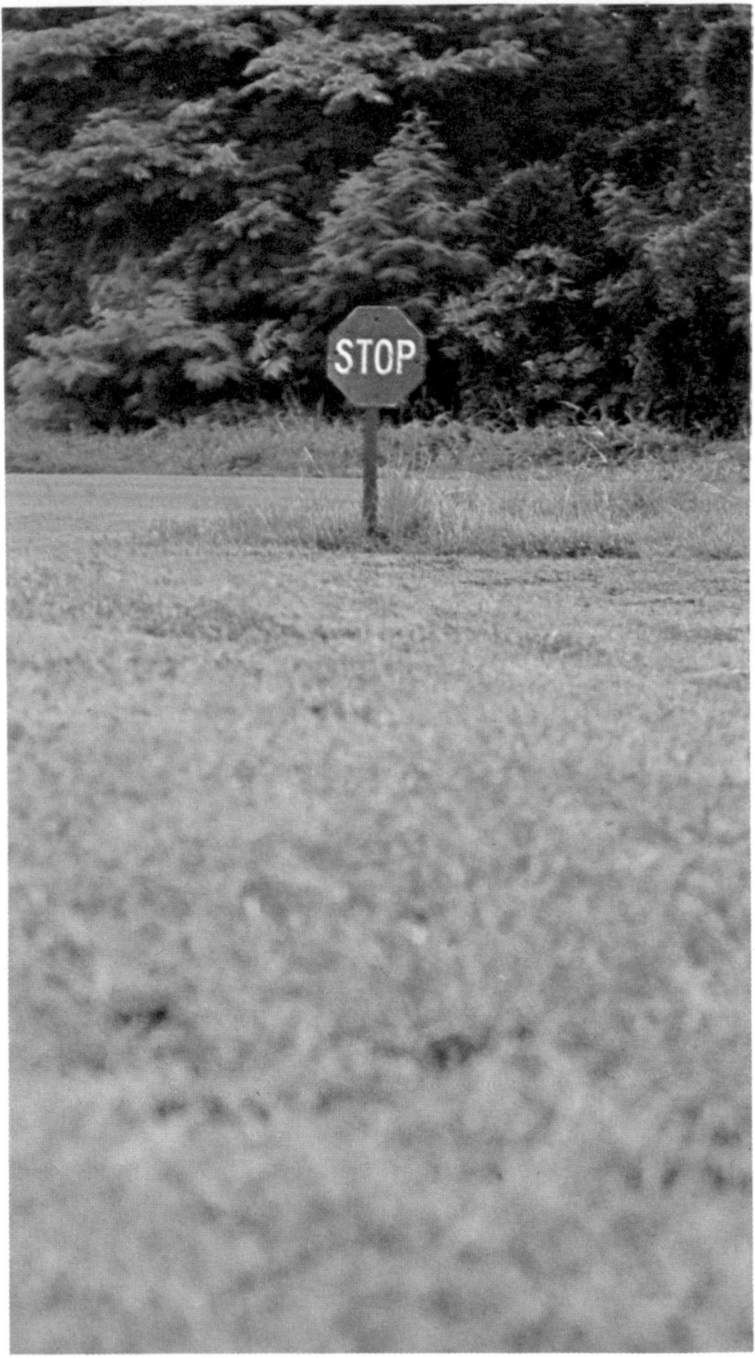
STOP

Today is the first day of the rest of your life.